A New True Book

AQUARIUMS AND TERRARIUMS

By Ray Broekel

This "true book" was prepared
under the direction of
Illa Podendorf,
formerly with the Laboratory School,
University of Chicago

CHILDRENS PRESS, CHICAGO

Photograph by Carolina Biological Supply Company

Amazon sword plant in a
tropical fish aquarium

*Aquariums and terrariums are of special interest to
the author. He has maintained many of them over
the years, and even operated his own fish store for
home aquarists.*

PHOTO CREDITS

Shedd Aquarium—4, 8

Jerome Wyckoff—33 (2 photos)

A. Kerstitch—10, 25

Louise T. Lunak—40

Miami Seaquarium—11, 13 (bottom), 16, 25
(left)

Allan Roberts—14, 18

Tropical Fish Hobbyist—22

Carolina Biological Supply Company—Cover, 2,
6, 7, 13 (top), 19, 21, 23, 24, 26, 27, 29, 30, 34
(3 photos), 35, 37, 38, 39, 42, 43

Cover—Goldfish and plants in a freshwater
aquarium

Library of Congress Cataloging in Publication Data

Broekel, Ray.
  Aquariums and terrariums.

  (A New true book)
  Includes index.
  Summary: Photographs and text describe marine
life displayed in public saltwater and freshwater aquariums. Includes instructions on how
to set up, stock, and maintain your own
aquariums and terrariums.
  1. Aquariums—Juvenile literature.
2. Terrariums—Juvenile literature.
[1. Aquariums. 2. Terrariums] I. Title.
SF457.25.B76   639.3′4   82-4428
ISBN 0-516-01660-1   AACR2

TABLE OF CONTENTS

Aquariums and Terrariums. . . 5
Saltwater Fish. . . 9
Freshwater Fish. . . 12
Other Animals. . . 15
Home Aquariums. . . 19
Babies Born Alive. . . 21
Egg-laying Tropical Fish. . . 23
Snails. . . 27
Plants. . . 28
A Saltwater Aquarium. . . 31
A Pond Aquarium. . . 32
Starting an Aquarium. . . 34
Home Terrariums. . . 36
Jar Terrariums. . . 41
Small Worlds. . . 43
Words You Should Know. . . 46
Index. . . 47

Diver at a coral reef exhibit at a public aquarium

AQUARIUMS AND TERRARIUMS

Where would you go to see lots of fish? You would go to a public aquarium.

A public aquarium has many fish tanks. You can see other kinds of animals, too.

Some people keep fish at home. The fish are kept in a tank. The tank is a home aquarium.

Aquariums have water in them.

Climate-controlled terrarium

Terrariums have soil in them.

Fish are kept in aquariums.

Plants are kept in terrariums. Sometimes animals are kept in them, too.

Diver feeding a nurse shark at a public aquarium

SALTWATER FISH

Many of the fish in a public aquarium live in salt water. These fish come from the oceans.

The dogfish is a saltwater fish. The dogfish is a kind of shark.

The cod is an important food fish. Many cod are caught in the Atlantic Ocean.

This saltwater fish does
not look like a fish. It is
the sea horse. It has fins
and gills. It uses its tail to
hold on to plant parts.

Some saltwater fish have very pretty colors.

The yellow tang is found in the Pacific Ocean. Many tangs are found around the Hawaiian Islands.

Tang fish are found in many colors.

FRESHWATER FISH

Many aquarium fish live in fresh water. They are found in lakes, rivers, and ponds.

There are different kinds of freshwater catfish. One kind is the blue catfish.

There are many kinds of freshwater sunfish, too. One kind is the green sunfish. Another kind is the black-banded sunfish.

Blue-channel catfish

Black-banded sunfish

Octopus catching crab

OTHER ANIMALS

Other kinds of animals can be seen in public aquariums. The octopus is found in some aquariums.

An octopus has eight arms. The arms are called tentacles. The octopus lives in salt water.

Saltwater turtles are known as sea turtles. They are bigger than freshwater turtles.

The green turtle is a sea turtle. It needs a large tank and room to swim.

Green turtle

You may see hermit crabs in an aquarium.

Some kinds of hermit crabs are found in salt water. They are kept in aquarium tanks.

Other kinds of hermit crabs stay on land. They are kept in terrariums.

Some hermit crab body parts, such as the tail, are

Hermit crab

soft. The crabs put those
parts inside empty shells
they find. Then the soft
parts cannot get hurt. The
crabs carry the shells with
them.

Photograph by Carolina Biological Supply Company

HOME AQUARIUMS

Many people keep small aquarium tanks in their homes or offices. The fish kept in them are called tropical fish.

Most home aquariums hold freshwater tropical fish.

But some people have saltwater aquariums. Different kinds of small saltwater tropical fish are kept in them.

Guppies

BABIES BORN ALIVE

Some tropical fish have babies that are born alive.

Guppies have their babies alive.

Guppies are freshwater fish. Grown up guppies are about an inch long. Guppies are easy to take care of.

Swordtail

Swordtails are freshwater fish.

Swordtails have their young alive.

A part of the tail fin of this fish looks like a sword. Only the male (father) swordtail has the sword. The female (mother) fish does not.

EGG-LAYING TROPICAL FISH

Some tropical fish lay eggs. The babies hatch from the eggs.

Zebra fish are freshwater egg layers. They make good aquarium fish. Zebra fish move quickly in the water.

Zebra fish

Photograph by Carolina
Biological Supply Company

Neon tetra

Neon tetras are egg layers. They are colored a bright, shiny red and blue. Neon tetras are smaller than guppies. Neon tetras live in fresh water.

Above: Flame angelfish
Left: Queen angelfish

Angelfish move slowly in
the water. Some of their
fins are long. They are
egg-laying tropical fish.

Some angelfish live in
fresh water.

Other kinds of angelfish
live in salt water.

Tiger barbs

Tiger barbs have black stripes and spots of orange on their fins and bodies. Sometimes tiger barbs nip the fins of other freshwater fish.

Photograph by Carolina
Biological Supply Company

In an aquarium snails are very important.

SNAILS

Snails help eat leftover food in an aquarium.

Most kinds of snails lay eggs.

The ramshorn snail is a good kind to keep in a freshwater aquarium. The ramshorn has a red shell.

27

PLANTS

Many kinds of plants grow under water. They need light to grow, just as do plants that grow on land.

Most aquarium plant roots grow down into the gravel at the bottom of the tank.

Some plants float in the water. So their roots float in the water, too.

Photograph by Carolina Biological Supply Company

Wash plants in clean water and put them into the
aquarium several days before you add the fish.

Little fish often hide
among roots of floating
plants.

Photograph by Carolina Biological Supply Company

Saltwater aquarium

A SALTWATER AQUARIUM

Some people have saltwater aquariums. Small fish and other animals can be kept in them.

Saltwater aquariums are harder to take care of than freshwater aquariums.

Plants do not grow well in saltwater aquariums.

A POND AQUARIUM

Ponds have fresh water.

A pond often has many living things in it.

Some of those things can be put in a pond aquarium.

Frogs and toads often lay their eggs in ponds. Tadpoles hatch from the eggs.

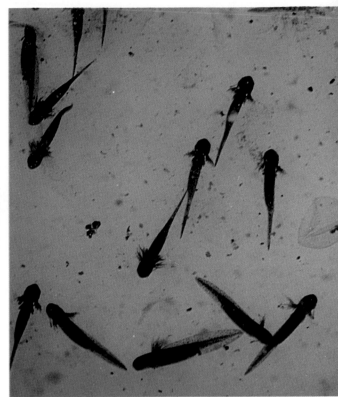

Left: A mass of frog eggs
Above: Tadpoles hatch from these eggs

A few small tadpoles are safe to keep in a pond aquarium.

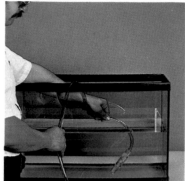

Above: Freshwater aquarium supplies include gravel, water filters, air pumps, plants, and fish.

Above Right: Always check to see if the aquarium leaks before you use it. Siphon the water out with a hose.

Right: Always pour water onto a heavy sheet of paper. This will not stir up the gravel in the tank.

Photographs on this page by Carolina Biological Supply Company

STARTING AN AQUARIUM

Many things are needed to set up a freshwater aquarium.

These fish are still in the water from their old tank.
To get the fish used to their new home slowly replace
the old water with water from the new aquarium.

This is how the aquarium looks when it is set up.

HOME TERRARIUMS

Terrariums can be made from many things. An old aquarium makes a good terrarium.

You will need some garden soil or sandy soil. Then you can add some plants.

You can put a hood and light on the top as a cover. Or you can use a piece of glass as a cover.

Photograph by Carolina Biological Supply Company

A woodland terrarium
has black soil in it.

Small ferns and mosses
grow well in a woodland
terrarium.

Other kinds of woodland
plants can be added, too.

37

A desert terrarium has sandy soil in it.

Cactus plants grow in the sandy soil. These do not need much water.

Photograph by Carolina
Biological Supply Company

Terrariums have plants in them. Animals can live in them also.

Wood frogs, lizards, and reptiles can live in a woodland terrarium.

Horned lizard or horned toad

Horned lizards can live in
a desert terrarium.
The frogs and reptiles
need to be fed and taken
care of. So do the lizards.

JAR TERRARIUMS

Old jars make good terrariums.

Put some soil in a jar.

Plant a few seeds in the soil. Then put on the jar lid.

Place your terrarium where it gets light.

SMALL WORLDS

An aquarium is a small world all its own.

So is a terrarium.

Living things are found in these small worlds. These living things need care.

This is a good small aquarium. It has goldfish,
snails, plants, an air pump, and filters.

Photograph by Carolina Biological Supply Company

All living things are worth this care. They are fun to watch and wonder about, too.

WORDS YOU SHOULD KNOW

aquarium(ah • KWAIR • ee • um) —a tank or other container where fish are kept.

cactus(CACK • tuss) —a plant with thick stems and spines that lives in hot, dry places.

desert(DEZ • ert) —a dry region usually covered with sand.

fern(FIRN) —a type of green plant that does not have flowers or seeds.

gravel(GRAV • il) —a mixture of pebbles or small pieces of rock.

Hawaii(huh • WHY • ee) —a state of the United States made up of a group of islands in the Pacific Ocean.

hermit crab(HER • mit CRAB) —a kind of crab that cover the soft parts of their body with empty shells.

hood —a cover that fits over an aquarium.

horned lizard(HORND LIZ • erd) —a kind of lizard with a short tail, broad, spiny body, and sharp spines on its head.

moss(MAWSS) —a type of small, green plant that does not have flowers.

neon tetra(NEE • on TET • rah) —a kind of tropical fish that is very colorful.

octopus(ok • tih •puss) —a sea animal that has a soft body with eight parts that look like arms.

ramshorn snail(RAMZ • horn SNAYL) —a kind of snail whose shell is shaped like the horn of a ram.

tadpole(TAD • pohl) —a frog or toad when it has just hatched and lives under water.

tentacle(TENT • ih • cul) —one of the eight parts of an octopus that stick out from its body.

terrarium(tih • RAIR • ee • um) —a tank or other container where land plants and animals are kept.

tropical(TROP • ih • kil) —a region of the world that is hot and humid.

INDEX

angelfish, 25

aquariums, 5, 6, 7, 9-35, 43

Atlantic Ocean, 9,

baby fish, born-alive 21, 22

baby fish, hatched from eggs, 23-26

black-banded sunfish, 12

blue catfish, 12

born-alive tropical fish, 21, 22

cactus plants, 38

catfish, 12

cod, 9

crabs, 17, 18

desert terrariums, 38, 40

dogfish, 9

egg-laying tropical fish, 23-26

ferns, 37

food fish, 9

freshwater aquariums, 27, 32-35

freshwater fish, 12, 20-26

freshwater tropical fish, 20-26

freshwater turtles, 16

frogs, 32, 39, 40

green sunfish, 12

green turtle, 16

guppies, 21

Hawaiian Islands, 11

hermit crabs, 17, 18

home aquariums, 6, 19, 20, 34, 35

horned lizards, 40

jar terrariums, 41

mosses, 37

neon tetras, 24

octopus, 15

Pacific Ocean, 11

plants, 28, 29, 31, 36-39

pond aquariums, 32, 33

public aquariums, 5, 9, 15

ramshorn snail, 27

saltwater aquariums, 9, 20, 31

saltwater fish, 9-11, 30, 25

saltwater tropical fish, 20, 25

saltwater turtles, 16

sea horses, 10

sea turtles, 16

shark, 9

snail, 27

sunfish, 12

swordtails, 22

tadpoles, 32, 33

tang fish, 11

terrariums, 7, 17, 36-41, 43

tiger barbs, 26

toads, 32

tropical fish, 19, 20, 21-26

turtles, 16

wood frogs, 39, 40

woodland terrariums, 37, 39

yellow tang, 11

zebra fish, 23

About the Author

Ray Broekel is a full-time freelance writer who lives with his wife, Peg, and a dog, Fergus, in Ipswich, Massachusetts. He has had twenty years of experience as a children's book editor and newspaper supervisor, and has taught all subjects in kindergarten through college levels. Dr. Broekel has had over 1,000 stories and articles published, and over 100 books. His first book was published in 1956 (it was published by Childrens Press).

DATE DUE

NOV 27 '84	FEB 14 '95	
JAN 16 '85	AUG 23 '95	
JAN 24 '85	SEP 15 '9.	
MAR 12 '85	MAY 12 '04	
MAR 15 '85	NOV 03 '04	
APR 29 '85	MAY 22 '06	
MAY 26 '86	NOV 28 '06	
MAR 25 '87	FEB 02 '7	
APR 06 '87	FE 05 '08	
FEB 4 '88	OC 13 '10	
SEP 13 '88	JA 13 '11	
NOV 27 '90		
FEB 7 '91		
MAR 17 '9		
MAR 17 '92		
JAN 06 '93		
MAR 24 '8		
JAN 23 '95		

GAYLORD   PRINTED IN U.S.A.